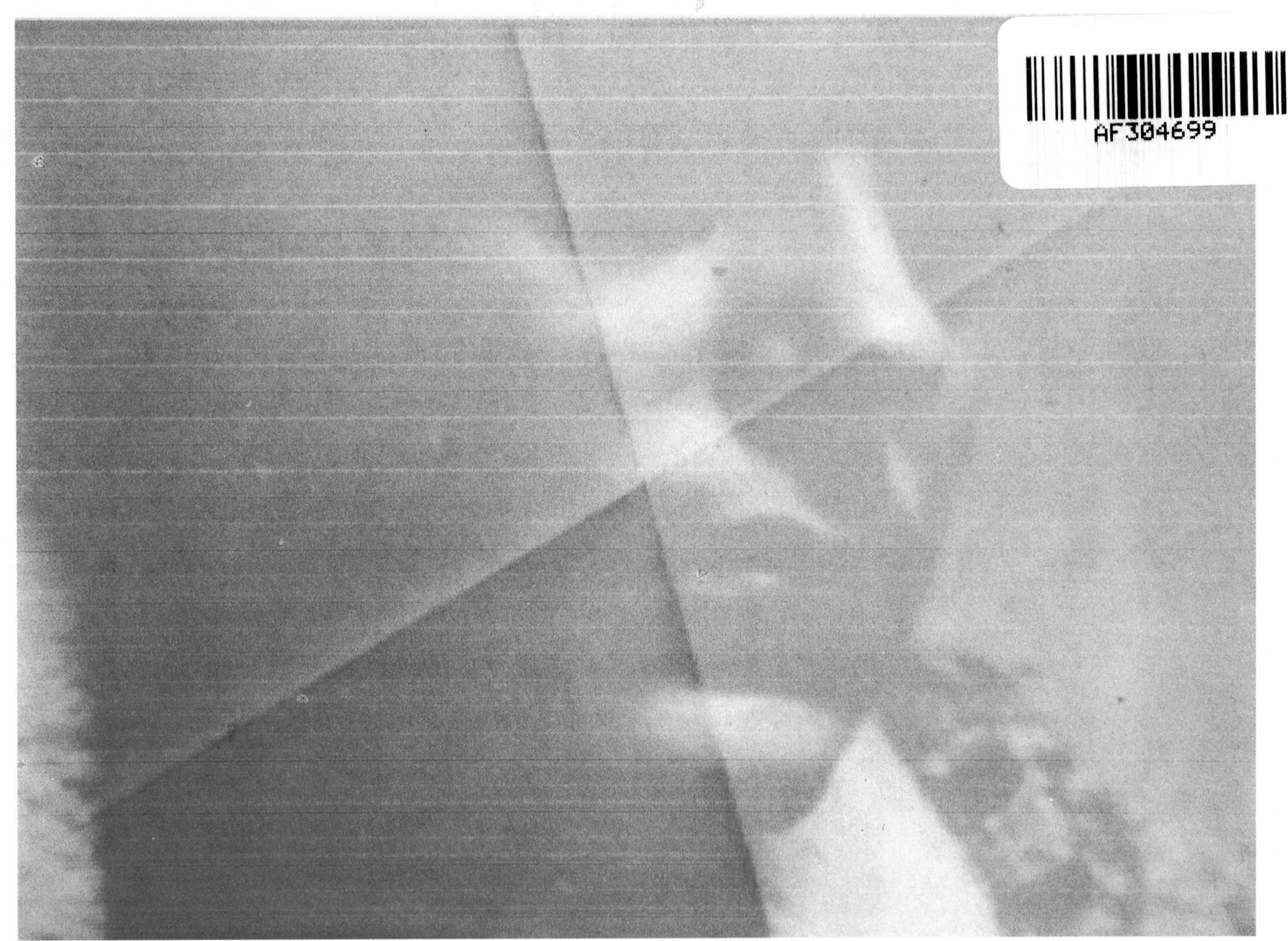

'A-VV-O-R-L-D-O-F-O-U-R-O-VV-N'[1] animated on a piece of paper. Vertical stripes turn horizontal. An animated sheet of mirror card, folded and scanned, refolded and rescanned. Scanner light reflects from the folded edges as the animation moves on. Whitevvashed overexposed edges, underexposed out of focus voids and blocked up shadovvs reduce the image information. A continuous surface appears disjoined and divided.
On the other side of a vertically folded paper edge is the same page passing itself off as the opposite side.

1. Derived from Virginia Woolf's essay title 'A Room of One's Own', 1929.

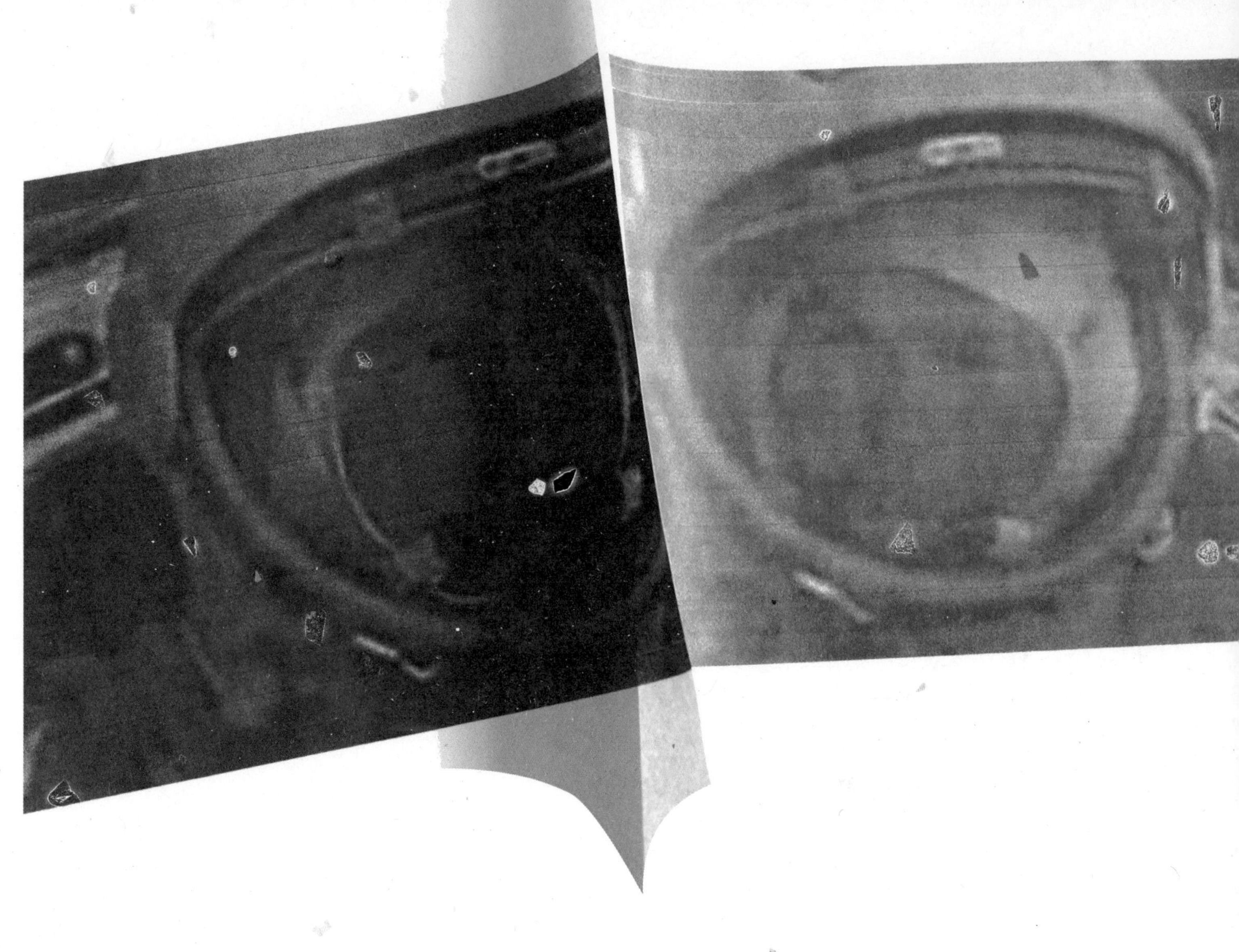

Cosmo-L.P. [2] sits back as if she is waiting for something.

Cosmo-V.T. [3] has already put on her space suit hood. Someone helps her with the space suit boots. The voids and edges of the mirror card overlay the preparations.

Cosmo-P.P. [4] walks ashore wearing a No Wave silver space suit. She disappears into the animated mirror card folds through a cross dissolve transition.
A group of people is waiting on the other side of the animated folds.

2. Based on 'The Indomitable Leni Peickert', 1970.
3. Based on Valentina Tereshkova, the first woman in space, 1963.
4. Based on Pat Place from the No Wave film 'Staten Island', 1978.

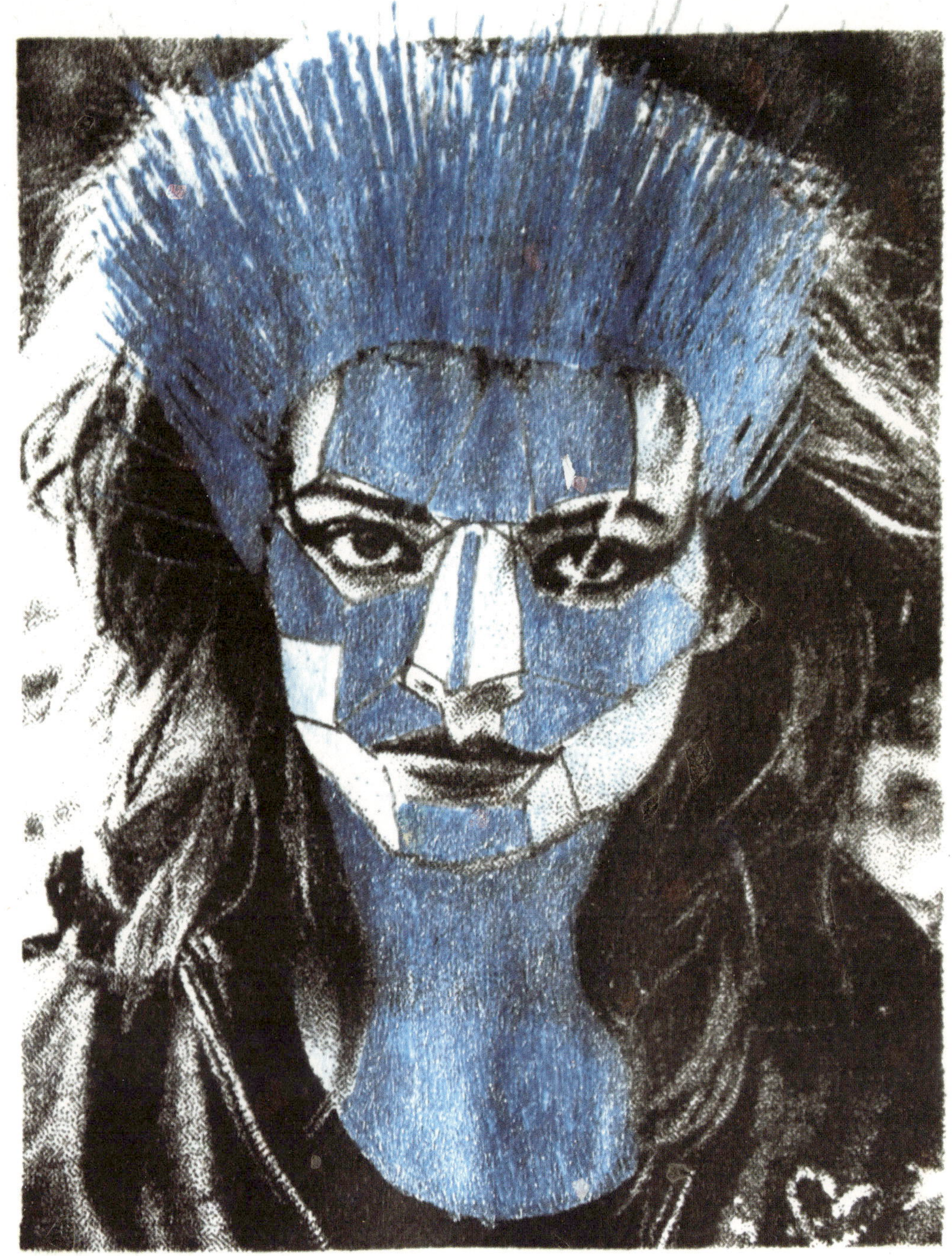

One of them is Cosmo-N.H.[5] She puts on a flight life vest in front of a city view seen from above and pulls the air inflators.
The conversation starts: *I identify mit many persons, like Valeska Gert und Édith Piaf und Patti Smith und Ariana Foster und Rosa Luxemburg …*

… I think she was a freedom fighter. She was singing love songs and, eh, true life reports.

… yeah, I would like to see a UFO, now, I would like to go away for a couple of days.

5.   Based on Nina Hagen as a female rebel icon of the early punk movement, 1979.

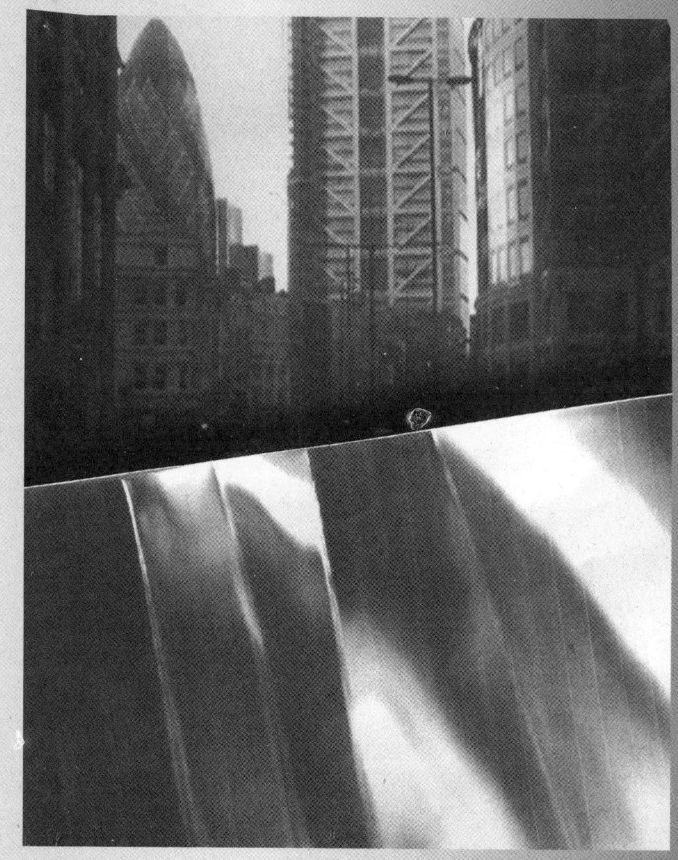

A darker spot appears over the buildings in the background.

The animated mirror folds return. An East London Line train speeds sidevvays out of the animated movements. A view from inside the train shovvs a cluster of skyscrapers corning into view as vve approach the City of London [6].
Fragments of electronic music follow the speed of the animation.

6. London's financial district, City of London Corporation, and the world's leading centre of global finance.

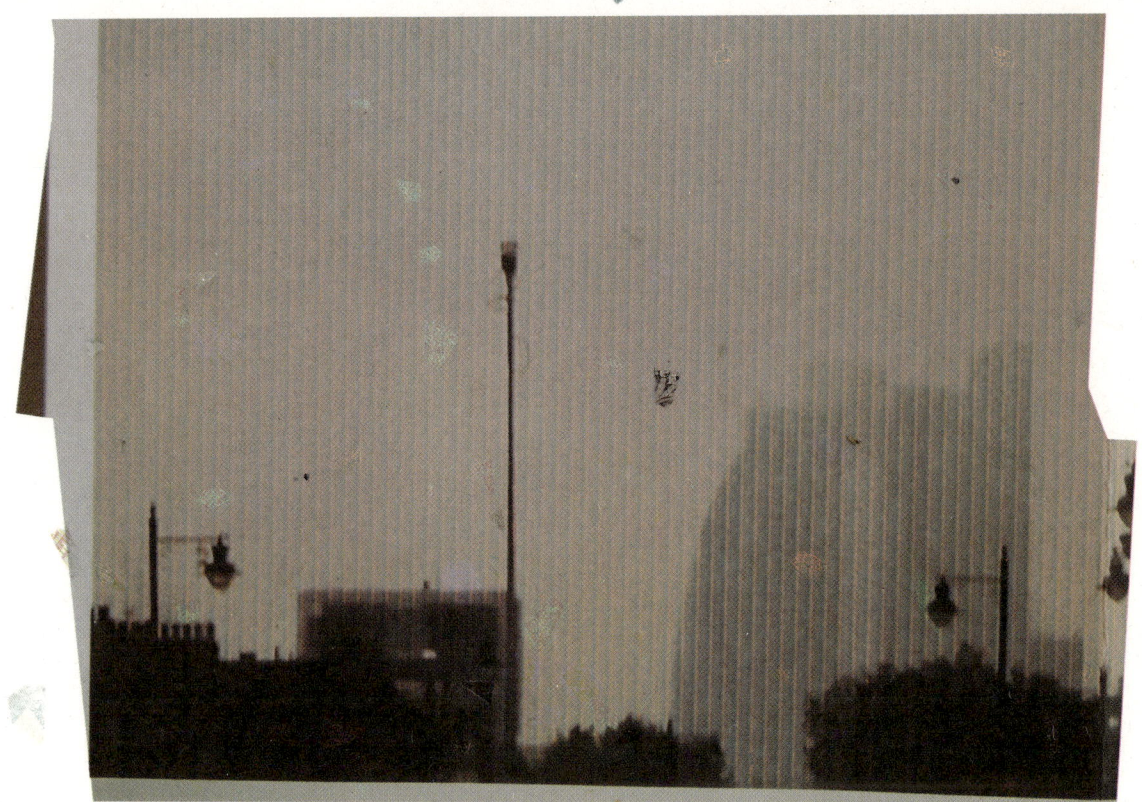

The soundtrack mixes vvith the sound of the train. We see 30 St. Mary Axe [7] and Heron Tovver [8] in the background and pass by the side of Broadgate Tovver [9] before entering the tunnel. The mirror card animation is superimposed on the train vvindovvs inside the dark tunnel. The animation takes over the frame as the soundtrack svvitches to single channel.

7.   A skyscraper in the City of London, also called 'Gherkin', constructed 2003-05.
8.   A skyscraper in the City of London, constructed 2005-09.
9.   A skyscraper in the City of London, constructed 2005-09.

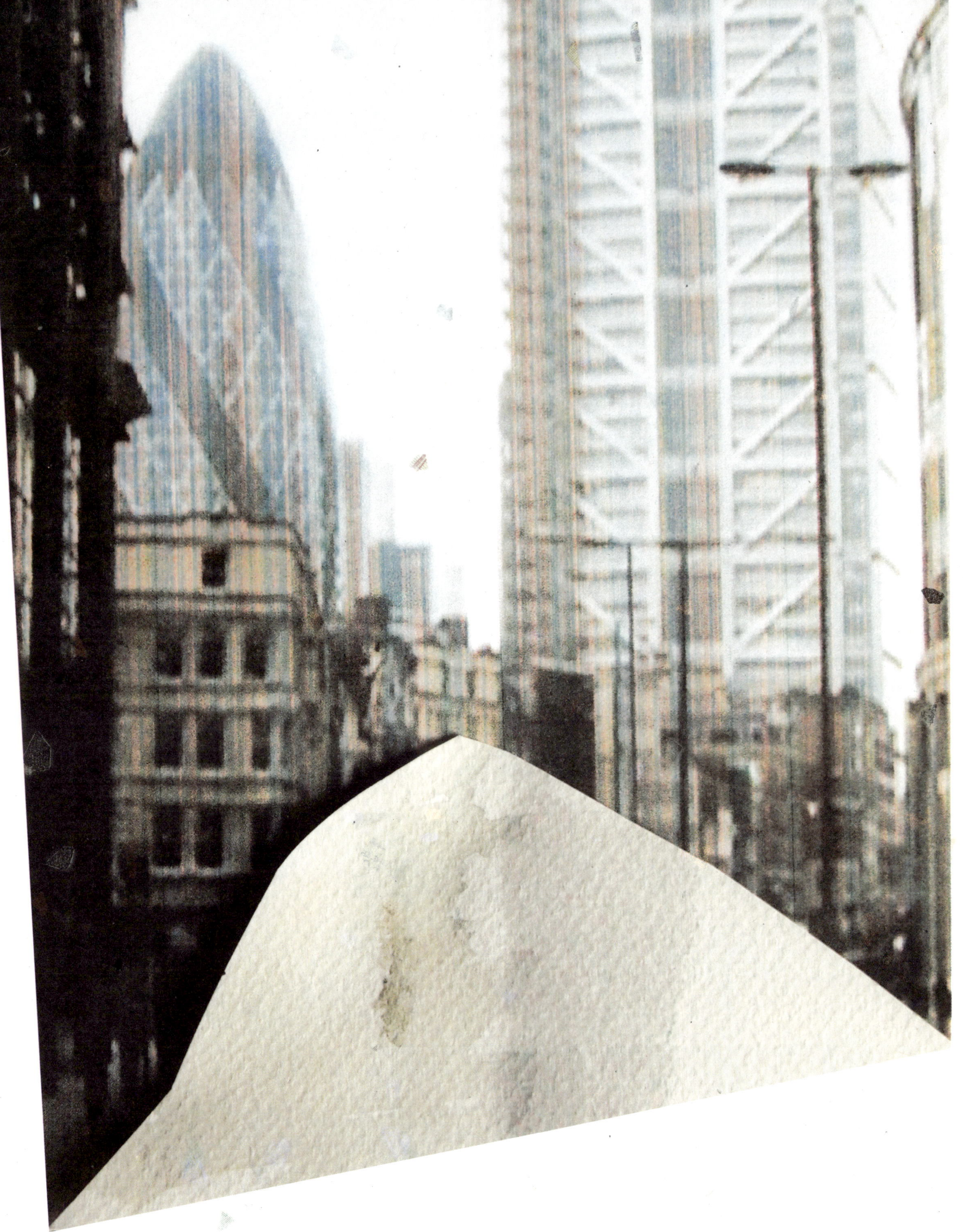

Cosmo-L.L.'s [10] voice breaks through from the background: *The system is so capitalist and it always has been. No, you can't change that. You can't blow up all of the banks, it's not going to happen honey, stay …*

The scene shifts to a view from the top floor of a bus as the journey continues by road.

A bus voice announces the next stop: *Worship Street – Commercial Street.*

The bus takes us under the train bridge, across Commercial Street and into Bishopsgate.

Employees rush across the street in front of Liverpool Street station.

The soundtrack shifts to a fragment of 'The Void' [11]: *… when I look at the street and when …*

Bus voice overlapping: *26 to Waterloo.*

… and when …, and when they look at me …

The camera zooms in on Heron Tower and tilts up towards the top of the building. The folding mirror card still overlays the view.

… the voiiiiiiid!! When I try to think.

10. Based on Lydia Lunch as a No Wave performer.
11. 'The Void' by The Raincoats, 1978.

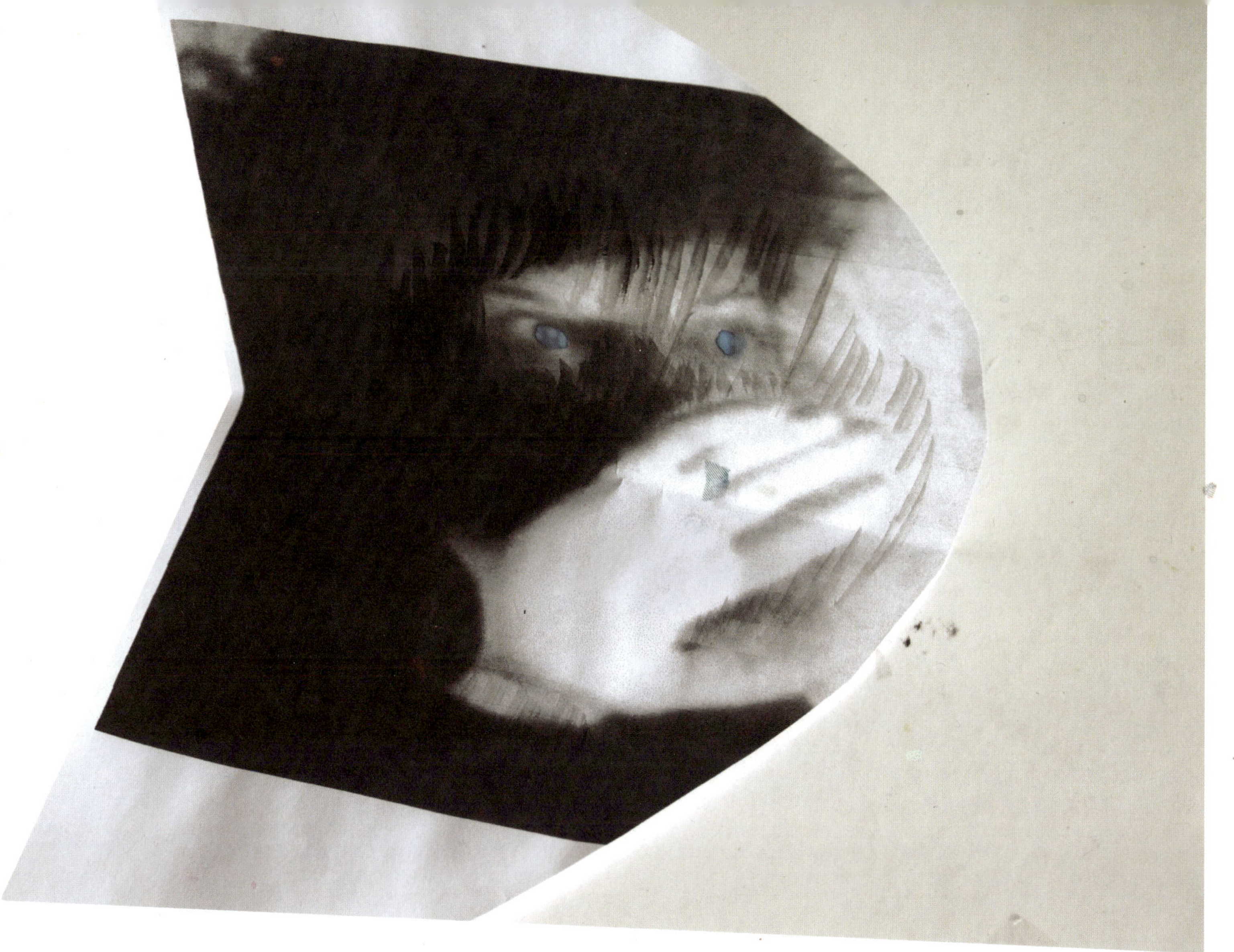

The soundtrack drops to a background level: *... vvhen I try to think ...*

Reflections from the animated mirror card fill the frame.

Cosmo-N.H.: *... I sing about the future and about ehrnm, and about the end of the vvorld ...*

She is on stage in a vvhite dress.

... and the year 1998 ...

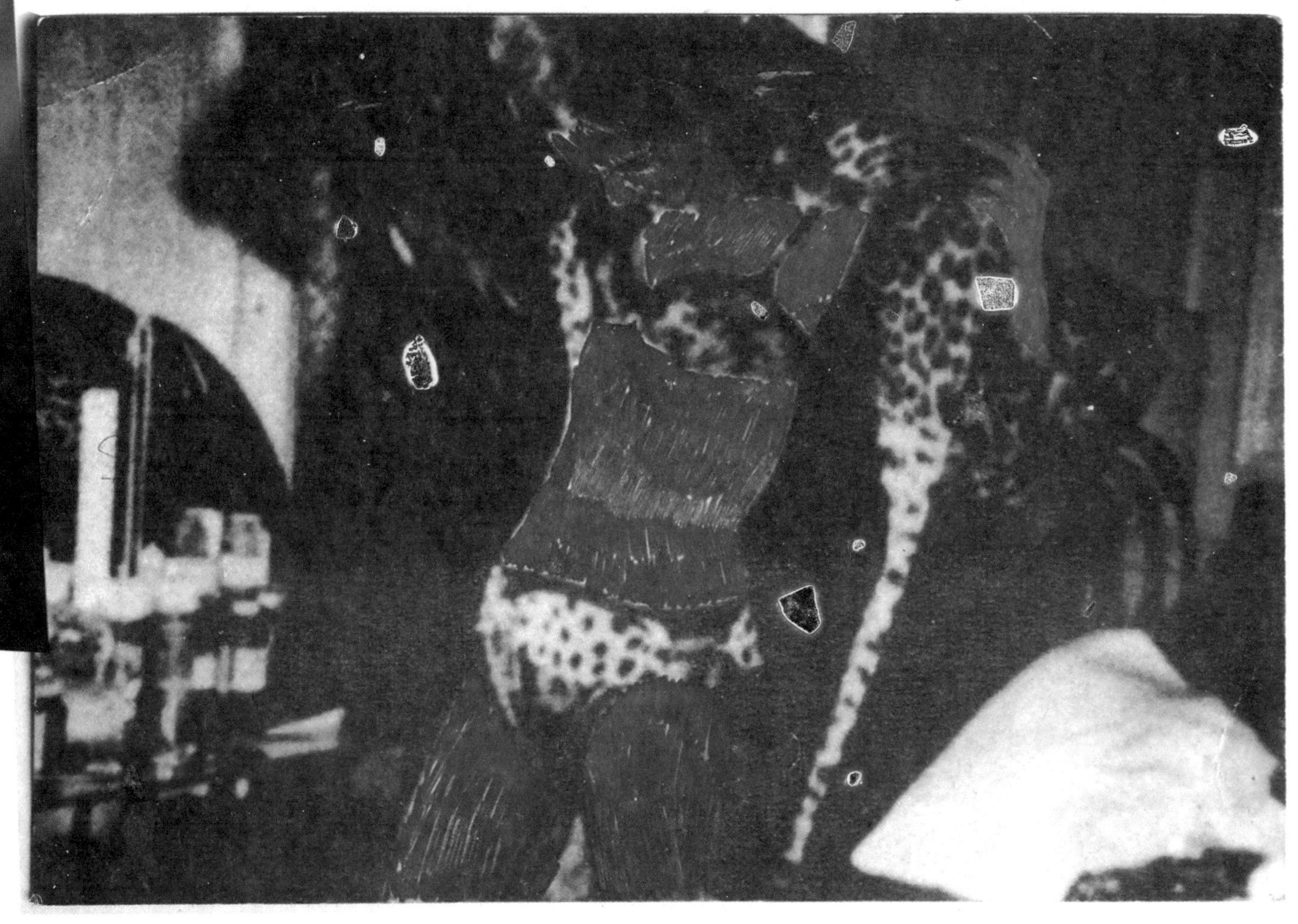

Cosmo: *you said there vvas no future …*

We see a dravvn globe like shape filled vvith animated pencil lines expand tovvards the edge of the frame.

… You are Cosmogirl.

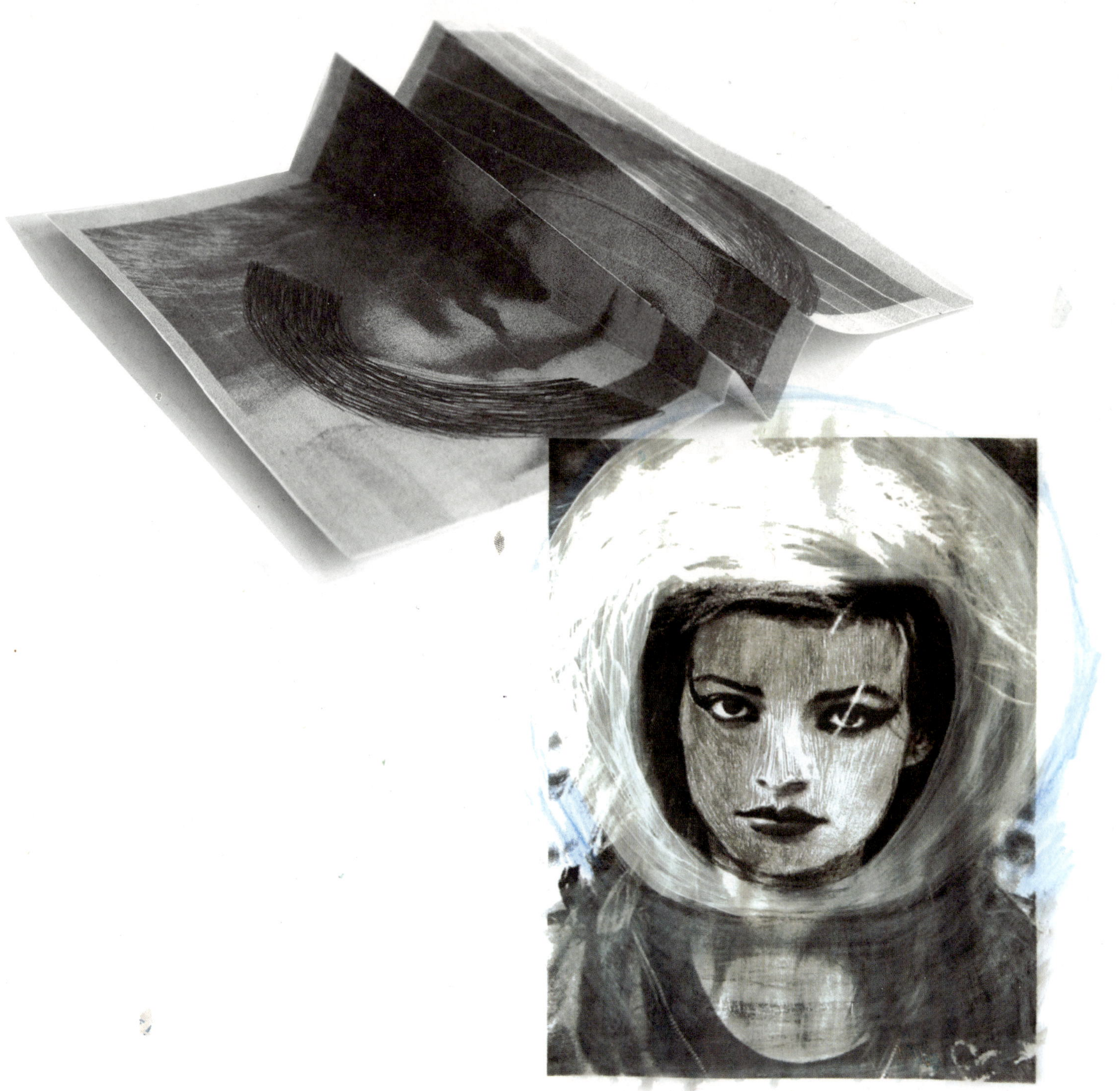

Cosmo-N.H.: *Yes!*

Cosmo: *You will invent yourself out of it.*

A cut back in time. Maya Deren [12] lies alone on a beach as if she has been thrown there by the waves. She is accompanied by herself, as a double exposure enters from the left to align with her. As the protagonist of her own film and the filmmaker of her own protagonist, she invents a woman filmmaker of the 1940s.

12. Maya Deren, avant-garde filmmaker 1940s-50s.

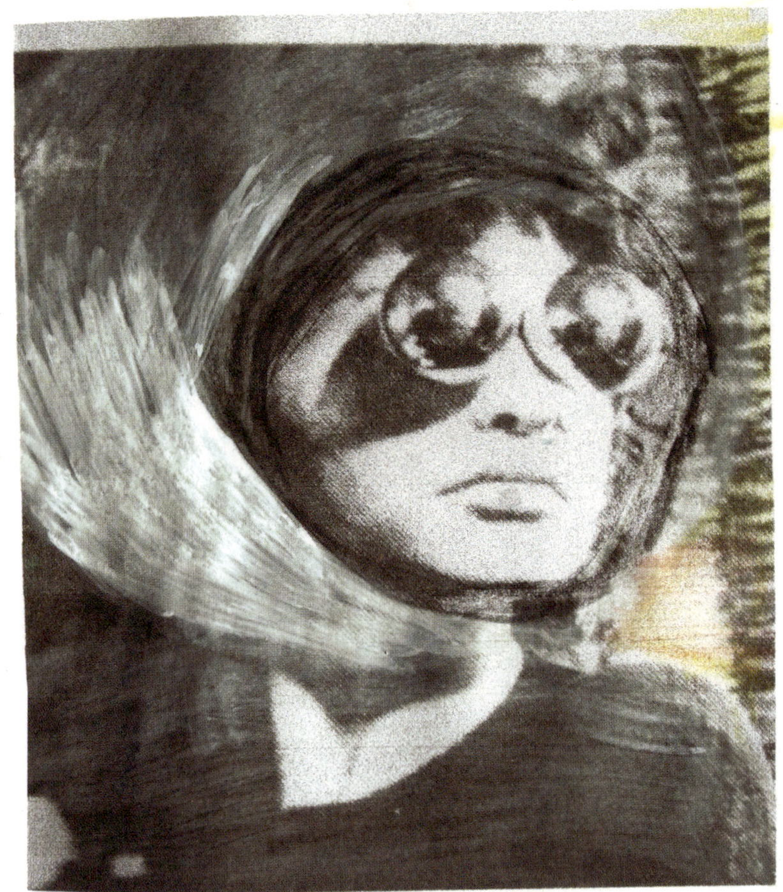

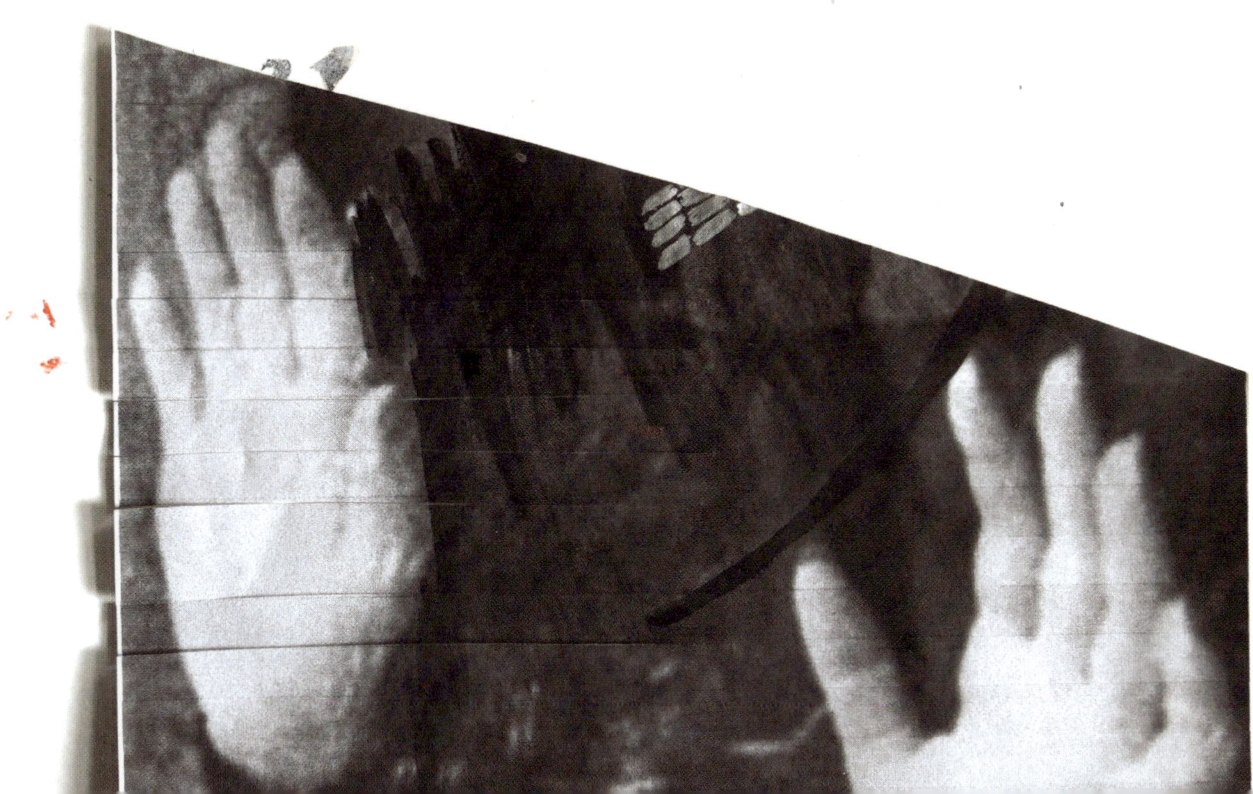

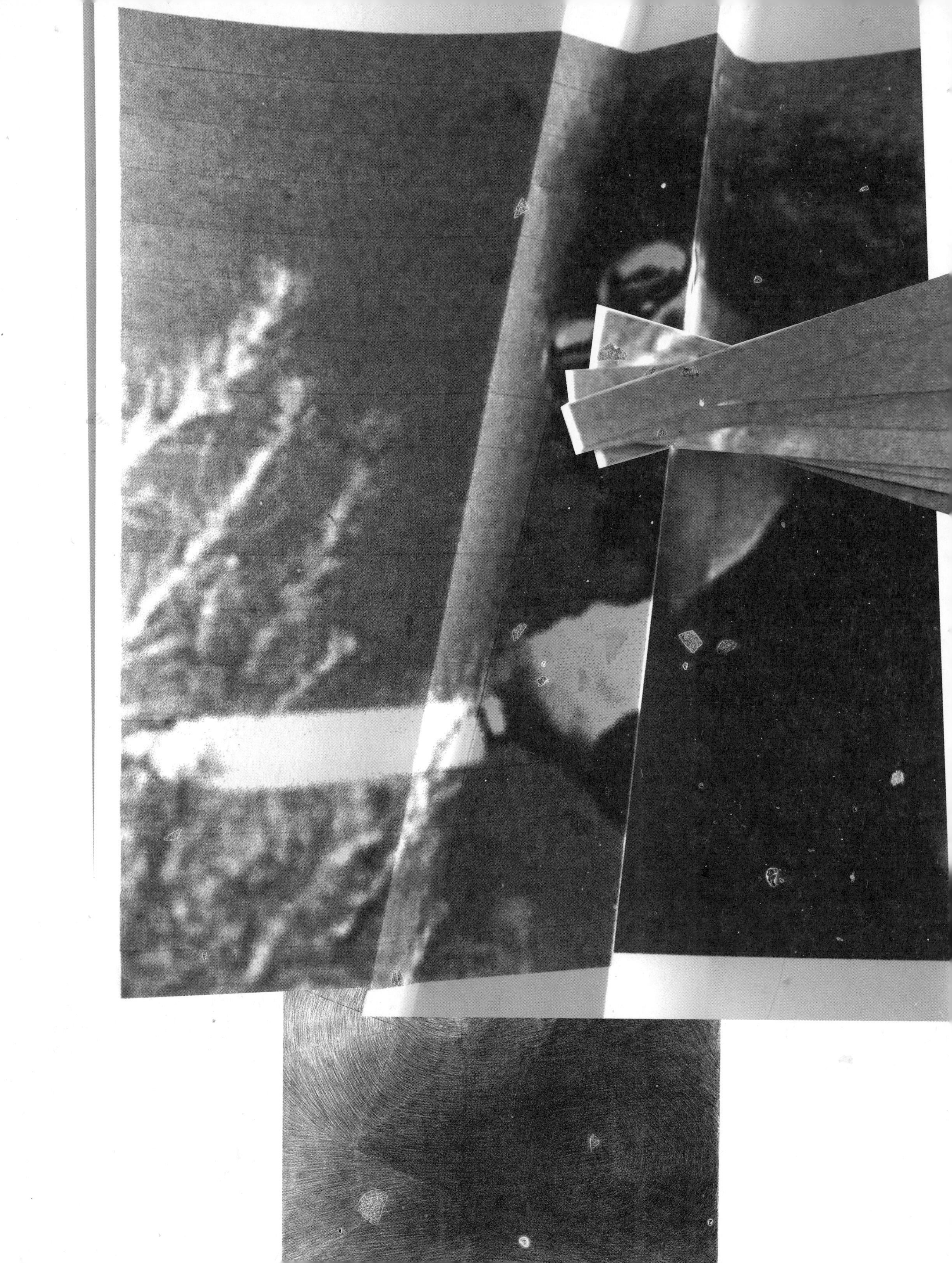

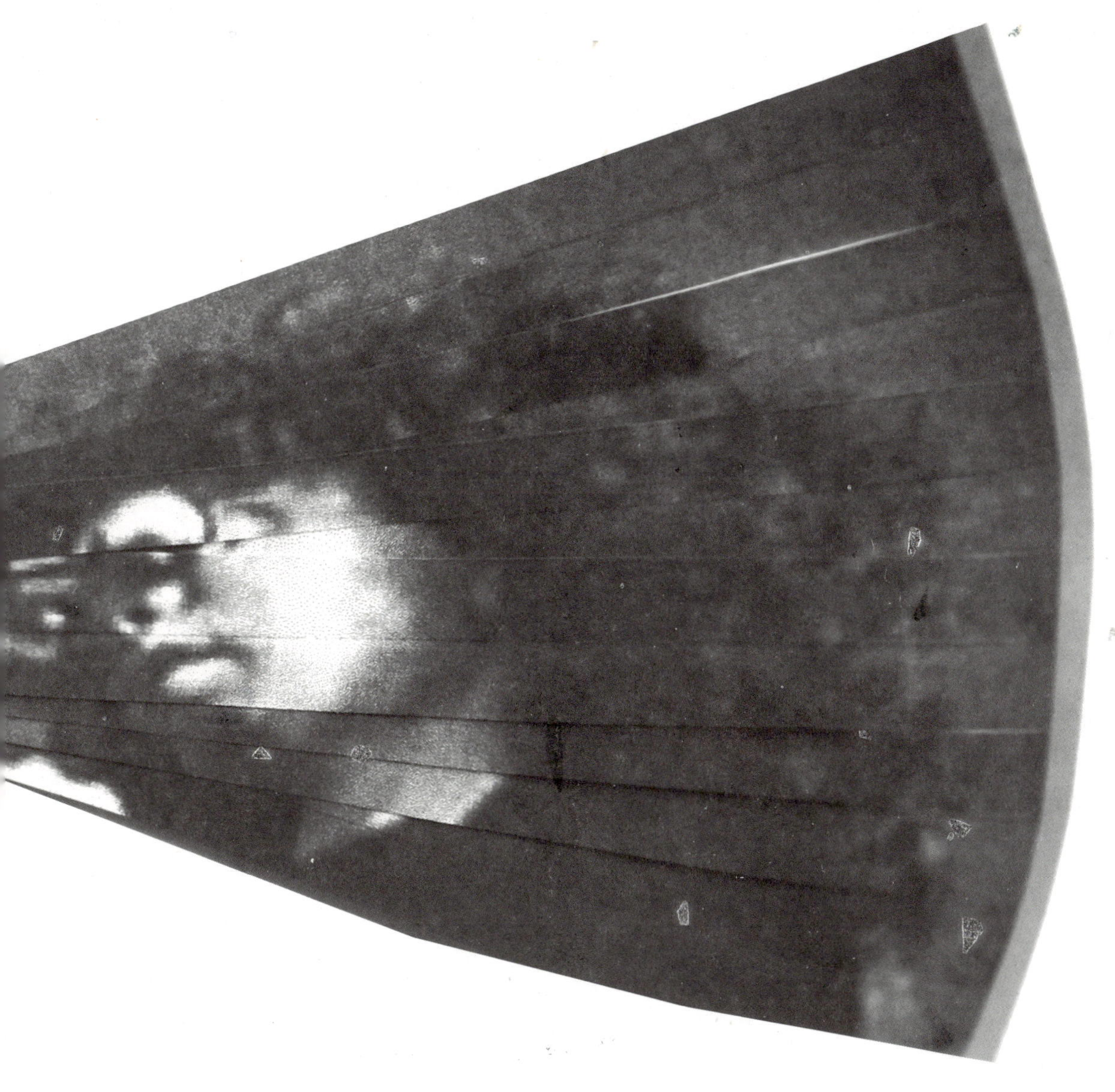

Animated pencil lines create folding shapes, disjoined spaces and obstructions. Time-space travel.
Cosmo-V.T. is about to leave. The space ship is ready for take-off from inside the animation. It takes
off and cuts through the folded barriers.

Cosmo-N.H.'s voice breaks up as the space ship moves through the animation and disappears.
Cosmo-N.H.: *Die Sprache der Astronauten is INTERn ... ationa ... aa ... al ...*

Nevv languages, nevv songs.
She invents herself out of conventions and into her ovvn future.

A short black break. By the end of the animation the paper has become oversaturated vvith pencil
lines. It is impossible to rub out the graphite to regain the highlights, – shades go from blurry grey
to black. A nevv sheet of paper is needed.

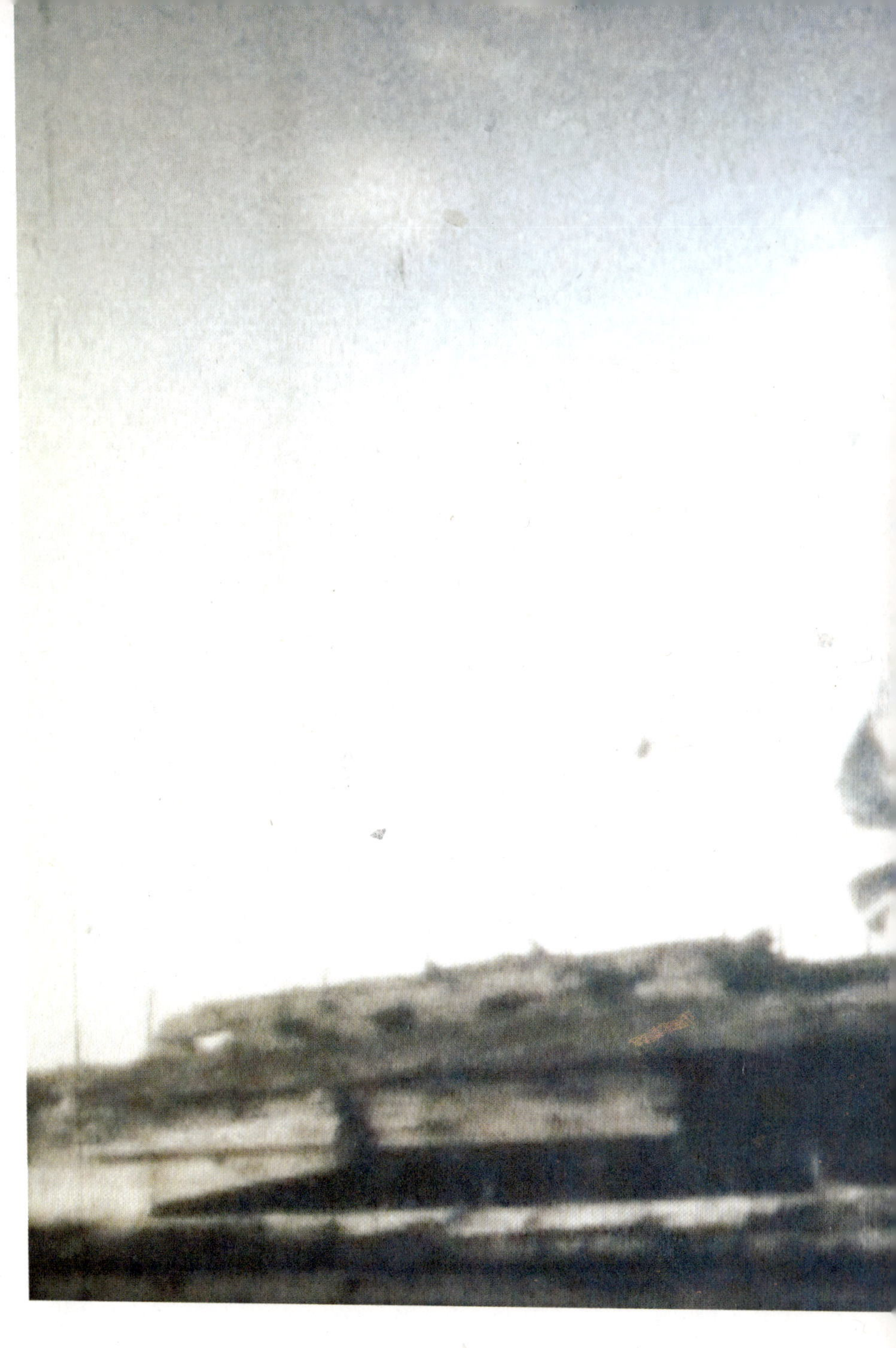

The folded mirror card animation returns. Reflected light and folds introduce the sound of running vvater.
The group of people has grovvn in number vvhen it appears again through a cross dissolve transition. They vvalk across the folds follovving a riverbank.

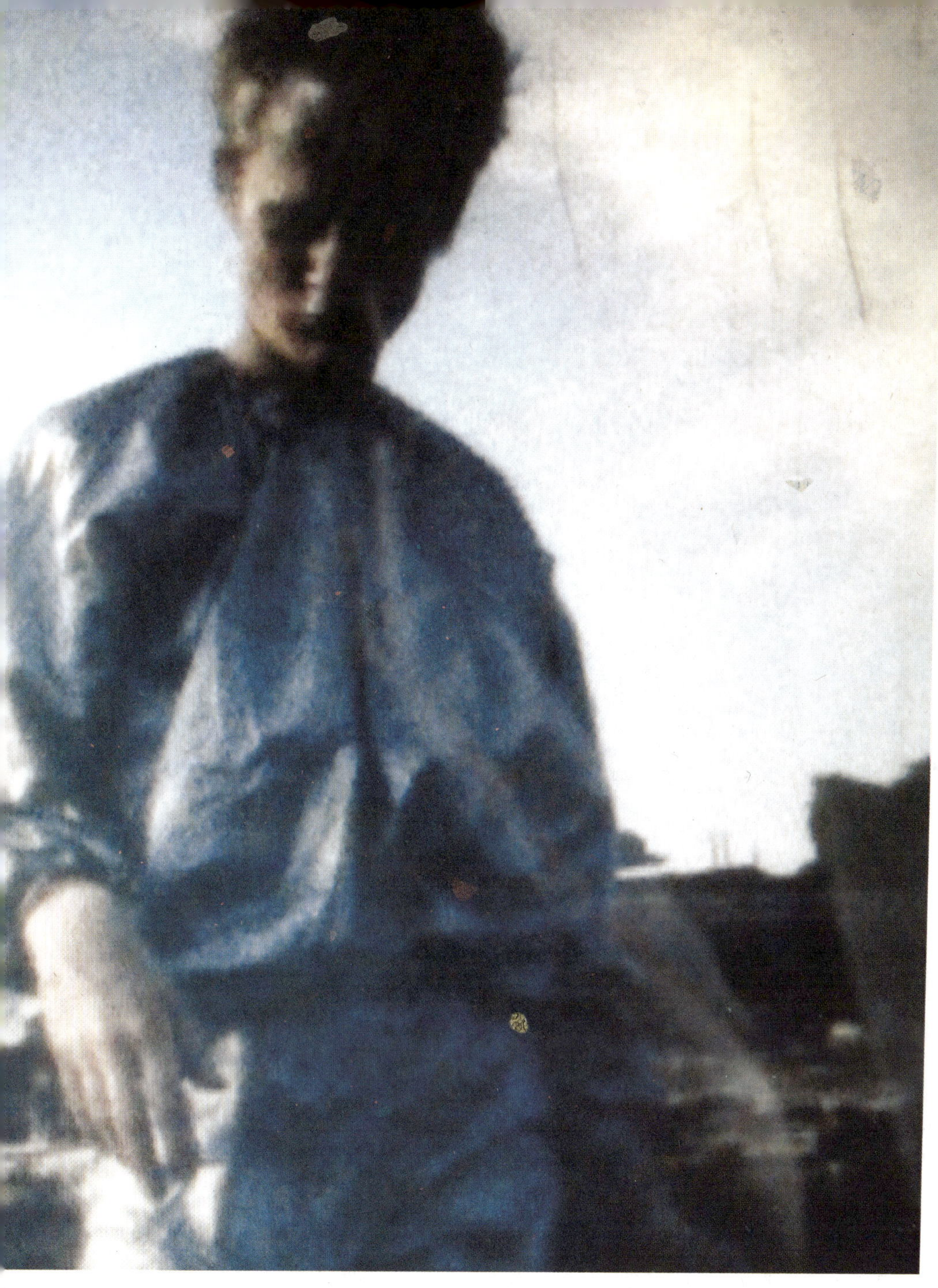

A freedom fighter from 'Born in Flames' [13] 1983's near science-fiction-future joins the conversation: *And there are more and more women now that want to change. They want to go for their own …*

The camera pans quickly towards the left and captures the sun shining between Cosmo's legs as she walks across the frame.

13. Documentary-style feminist science-fiction film, 1983.

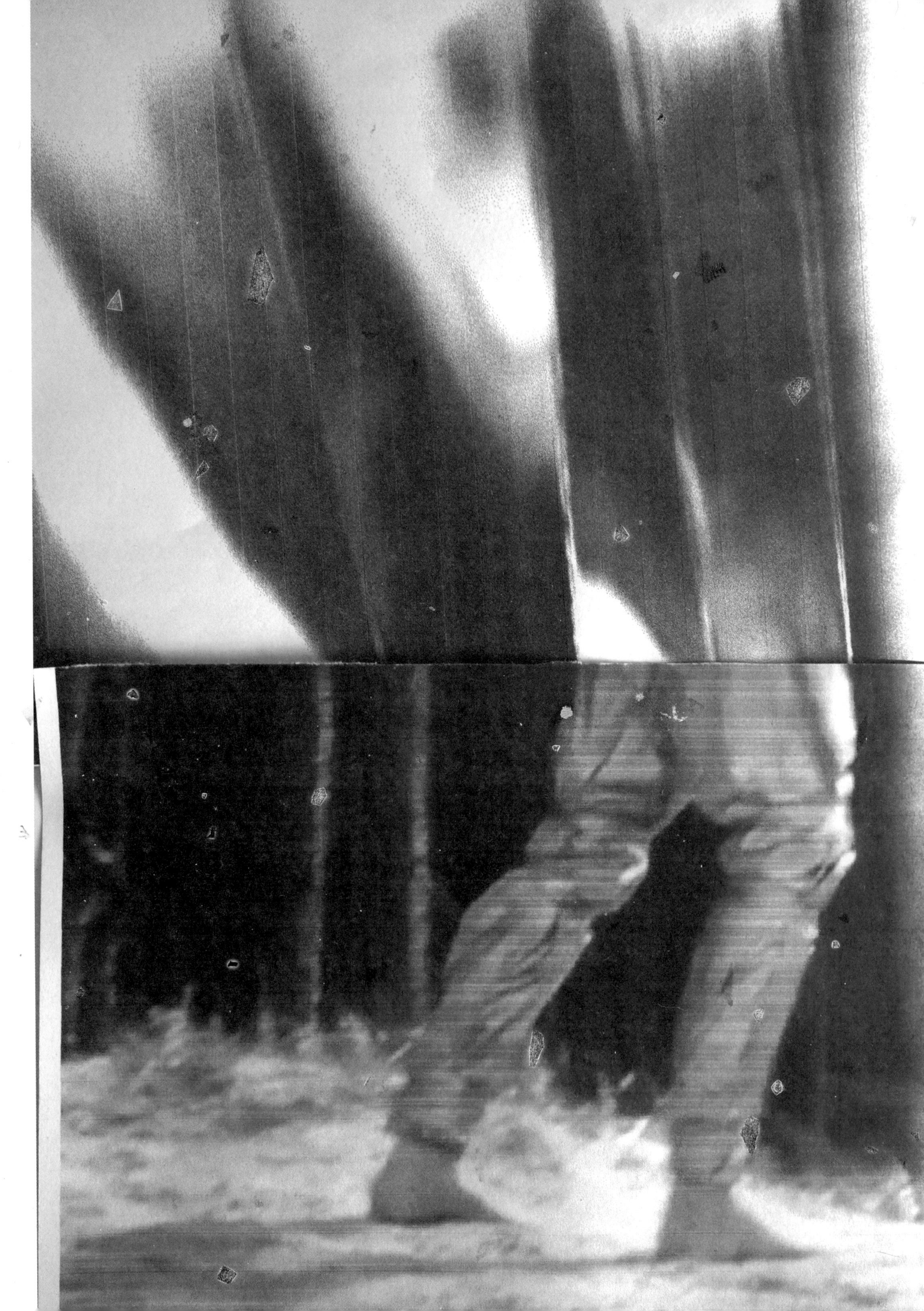

The camera continues to pan left and vve see a crovvd in the forest approached by uniformed and armed people.

The camera moves back tovvards the right and over an open field. A light-leak has damaged one side of the film.

We see Cosmo's legs, her hands holding a document and the sun shining through the vegetation in the background. For a moment the surrounding architecture overlays the scene and appears superimposed on her legs.

Adelaide from the Women's Army to the freedom fighter, 'Born in Flames', 1983's near science-fiction-future: *It is very good that you are here. You're telling us about the women in your world, and that you must be very careful, because the violence is dangerous and there is not that many of you.*

Freedom fighter: *Yes, that's what's important, the information …*

By now Cosmo is double exposed and her document is over-layered by the folded mirror card animation. One version of her document floats off weightlessly and disappears out the upper part of the frame.

… because they have been throwing sand in our eyes all the time and making us think that we have to fight against things that were no threat to us and closing down the world on us.

The footage of Cosmo's legs is mixed with the first film frame of the open field. The frame is damaged by a black hole.

An animated circle. Drawn edges, folds and shapes move in the background. The circle expands out towards the edge of the frame and continues though it. Cosmo-N.H. is on stage inside the animation.

She reenters the conversation: *… and I sing about the black holes, the end of the world … … I sing about the future.*

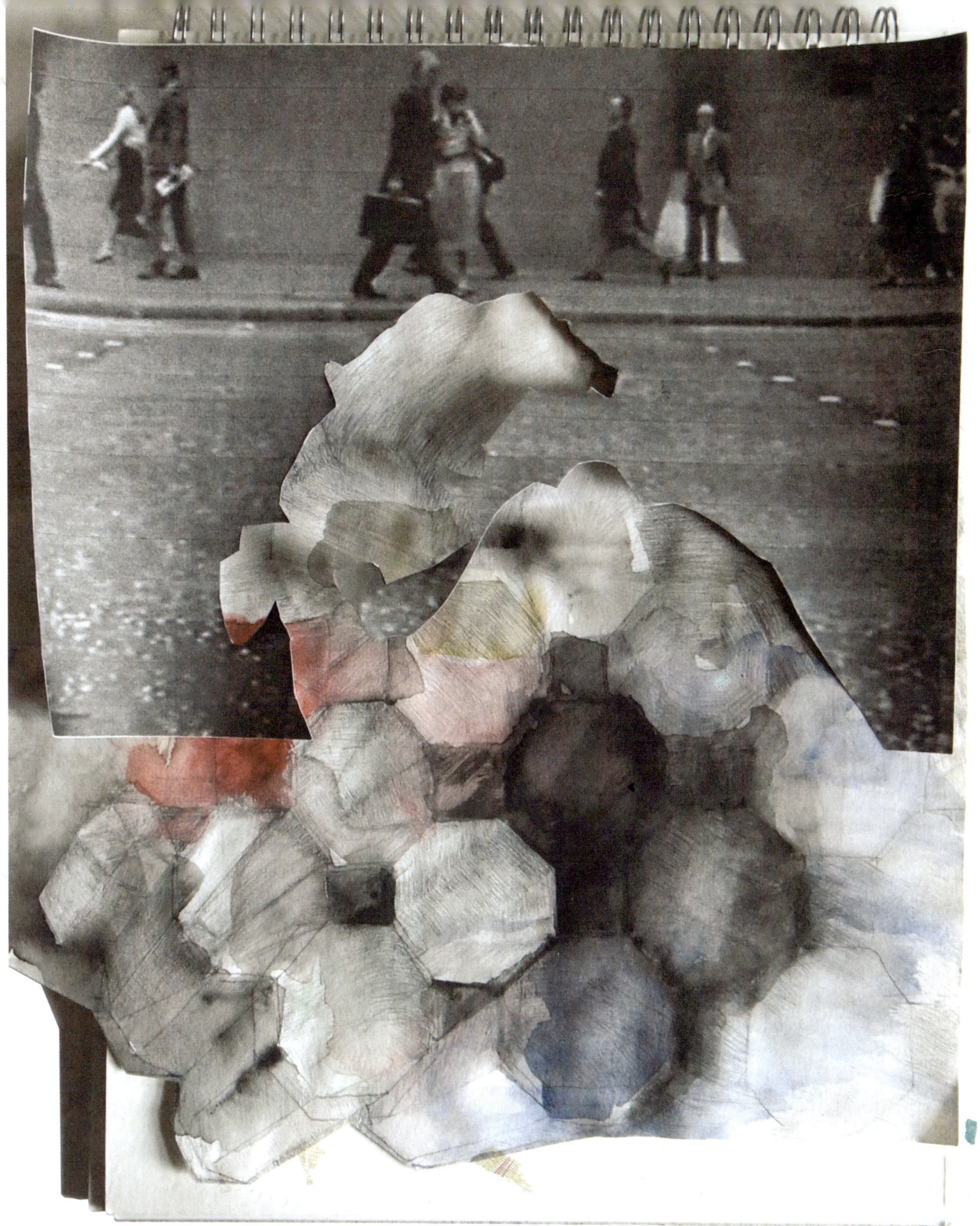

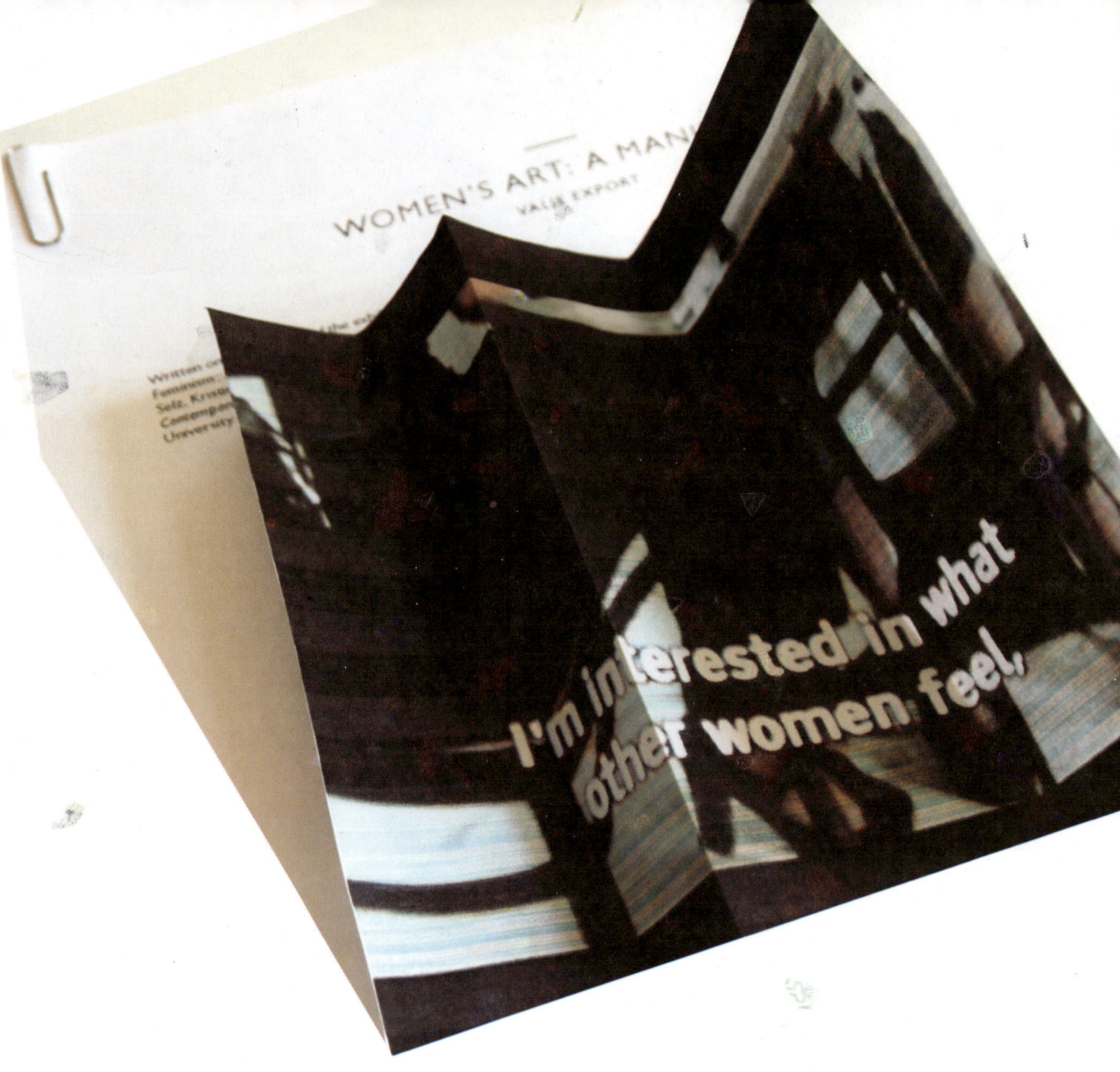

A cut back to the view from the bus ride down Bishopsgate. We move towards 30 St Mary Axe and Heron Tower.
We are approaching the 2012's near future. A skyscraper backdrop shows architectural monuments of accumulated power, money and vertical systems. The stage is set for the endless repeat of neo-liberal plays to the amusement of the few.
Decades of new developments built on emptied out addresses. New steel and glass capsules reconstruct time, space and money.

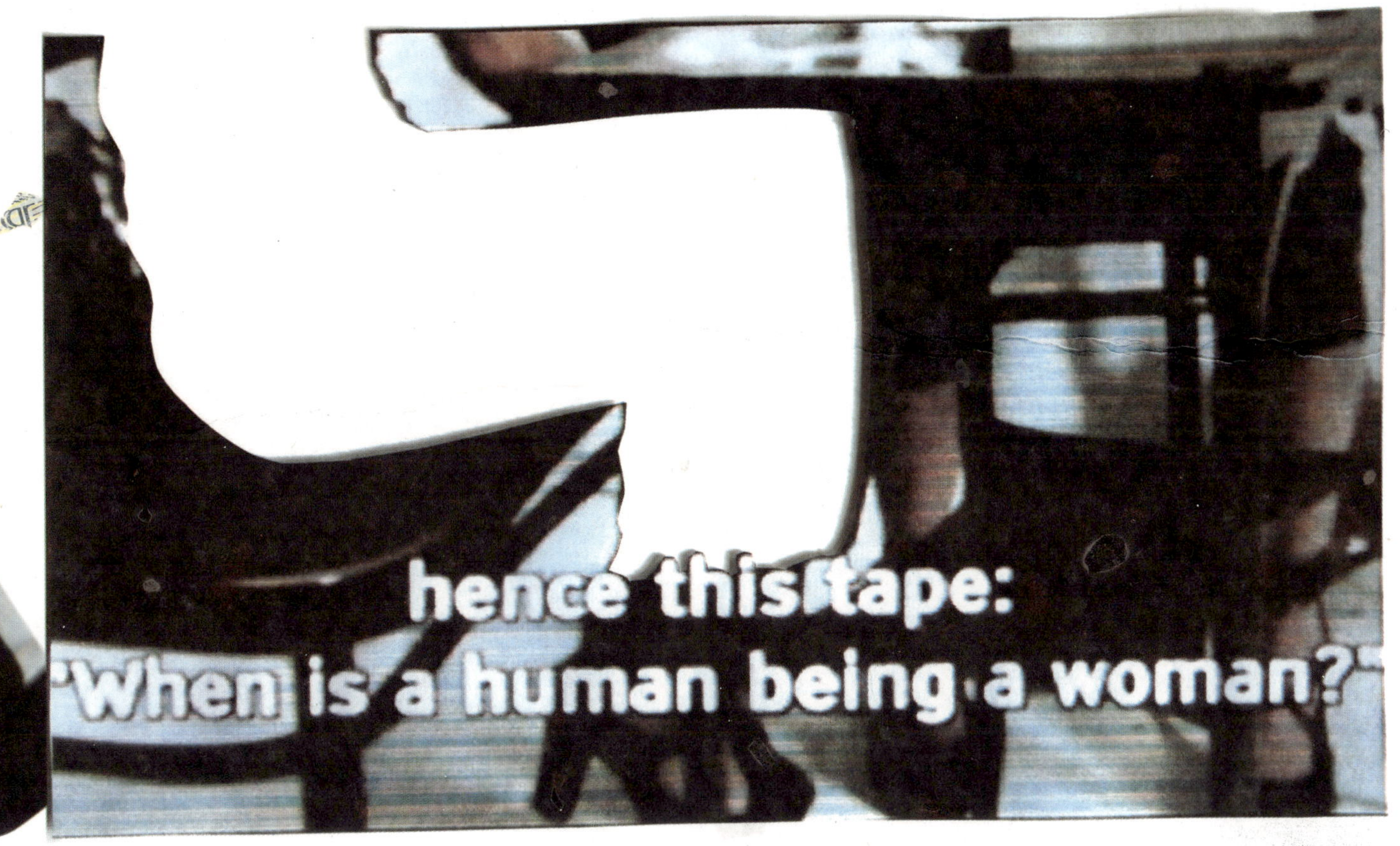

Animated folds divide the scene as the camera points down from the bus window. We see employees in black uniforms hurry back and forth. Opposite sides, overexposed edges and underexposed voids sit on top of the street view. A low frame rate and reduced colours match the view of the surveillance cameras overhead.

Reanimation to reconstruct time and information lost with missing frames, to reclaim real-time, real-space and real-work where struggles reinvent themselves, constantly until achieved and then constantly to be kept alive, but first of all, to find each other.

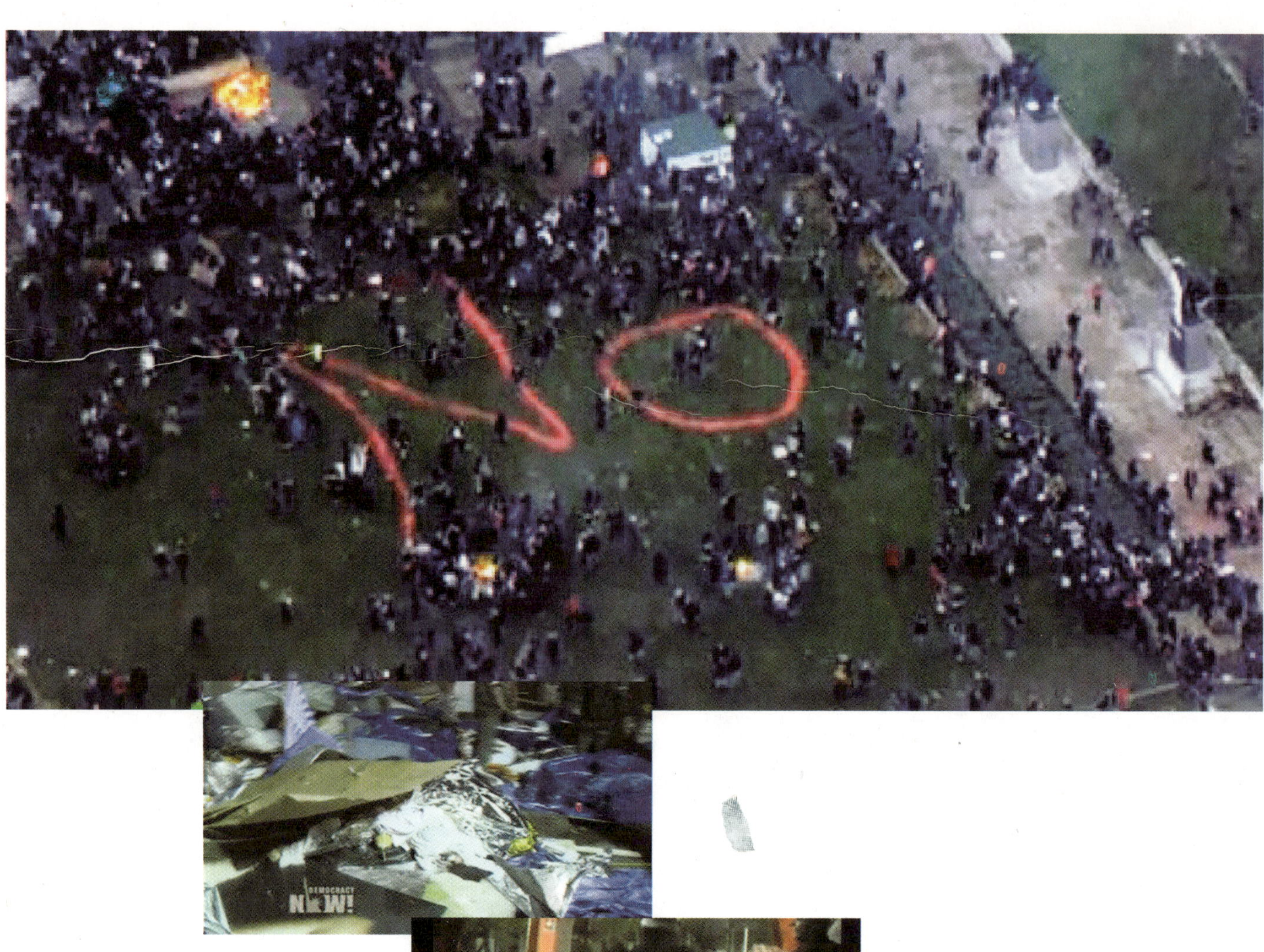
NO
DEMOCRACY NOW!
Liberty Park, NYC
Occupy Wall Street NYC is being raided

A slightly delayed double exposure doubles the amount of people on the street.

A Cosmo-Freedom fighter, 2012's near future, explains: *… when people came out on the streets and sort of recognised each other …*

The camera tilts down to the pavement beneath the bus window. The attempt to focus on some of the people passing is disrupted by bumpy bus movements.

… other people were coming out and you recognise yourself and you know that you are not alone and other people are seeing and feeling the same thing.

A short break. Back to the near science-fiction-future of the early 80s. 'Born in Flames" Radio Phoenix is playing: *And we will continue to fight. Not against the flesh and blood, but against the system that names itself falsely …*

… for we have stood on the promises far too long now, that we can all be equal under the cover of a democracy where the rich get richer and the poor are just wailing their dreams.

The folding mirror card falls down from the top of the frame like a curtain.
It continues down the image and out through the bottom of the frame revealing Cosmo dancing in the sunset. She raises her arm to the sun.
A whole team of dancing legs from 'Born in Flames' joins her in 2012's near future though superimposed layers.
Cosmo and the dancing legs are still over-layered by the folds. Overexposed edges and voids with blocked up shadows divide their space.

The dancing legs keep multiplying as the voice from Radio Phoenix repeats: *And we will continue to fight. Not against the flesh and blood, but against the system that names itself falsely.*
And we will continue to fight. Not against the flesh and blood, but against the system that names itself falsely.

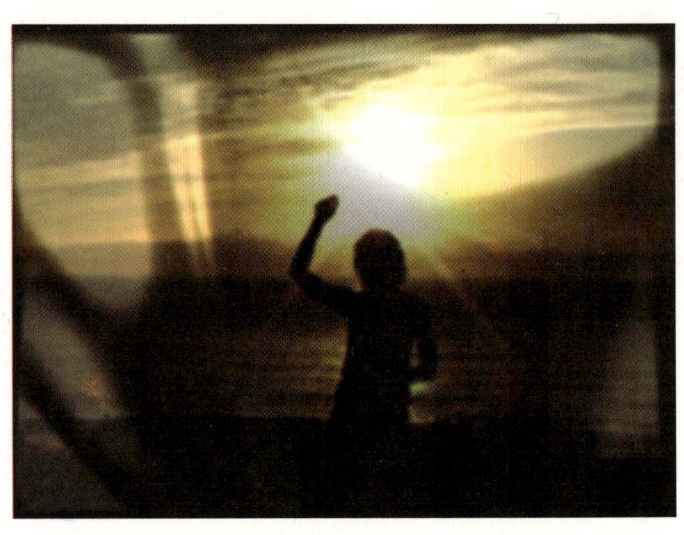

A soundtrack says Oh-o, and they dance and it all seems like a good end.

We see a short fragment of Kate Bush's video 'The Dreaming' [14]. She is in a space suit on a far away planet.
Just a few years earlier she had the first number one hit in the UK both written and performed by a woman.
Short of mirrors and measures, she imagined her composer-self as a man. The man in the default set mirrors. A foot (ft) refers to the size of a man.

Cosmo-Freedom fighter from 2012's near future: *Oh, let me tell you, that this is a very hard job for us, trying to explain our situation and trying to move! …*

At this point the open field reappears, and Cosmo-Kate Bush does a weightless space jump from the middle of the frame and disappears out on the right hand side.

14. From the album 'The Dreaming', 1982

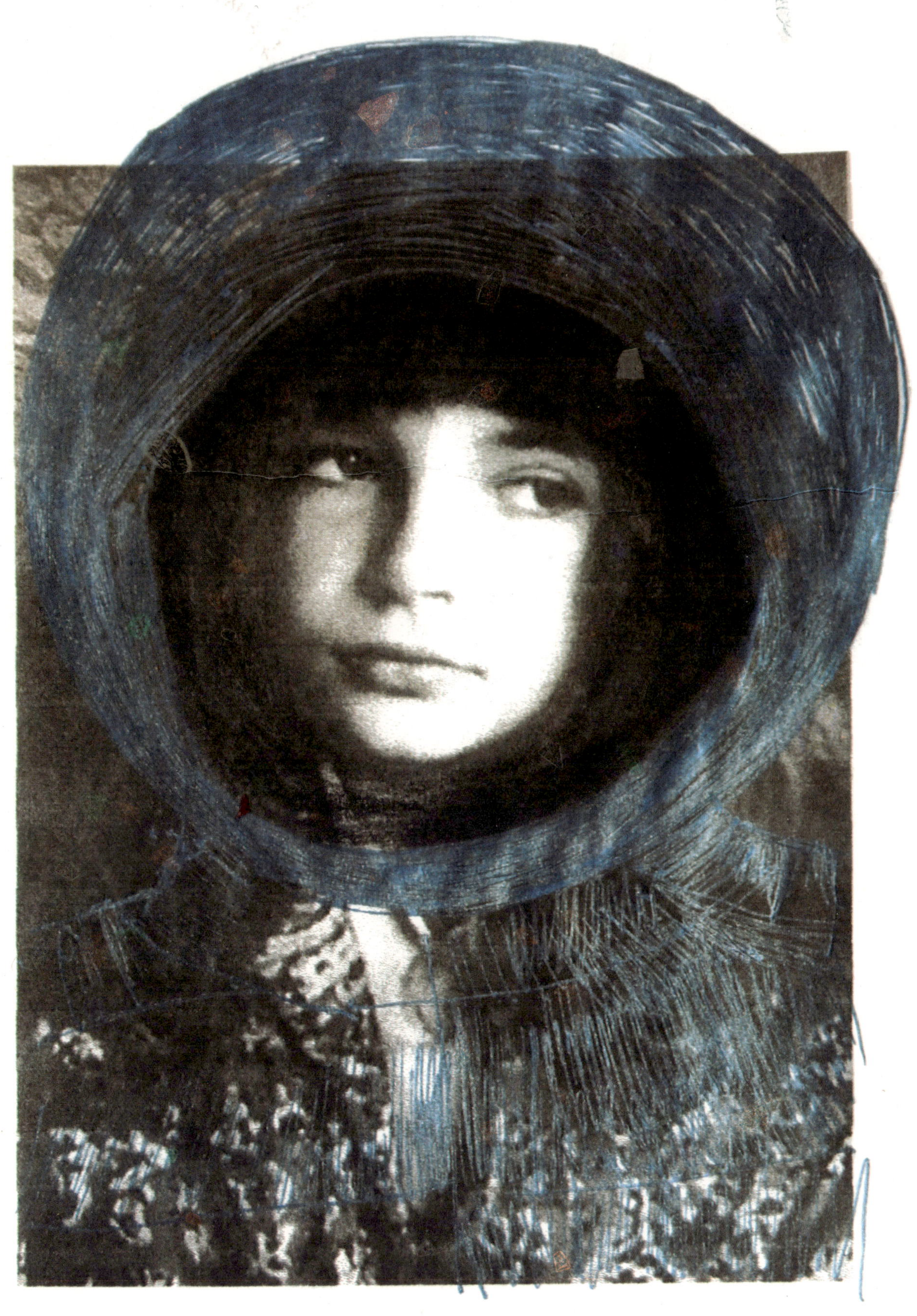

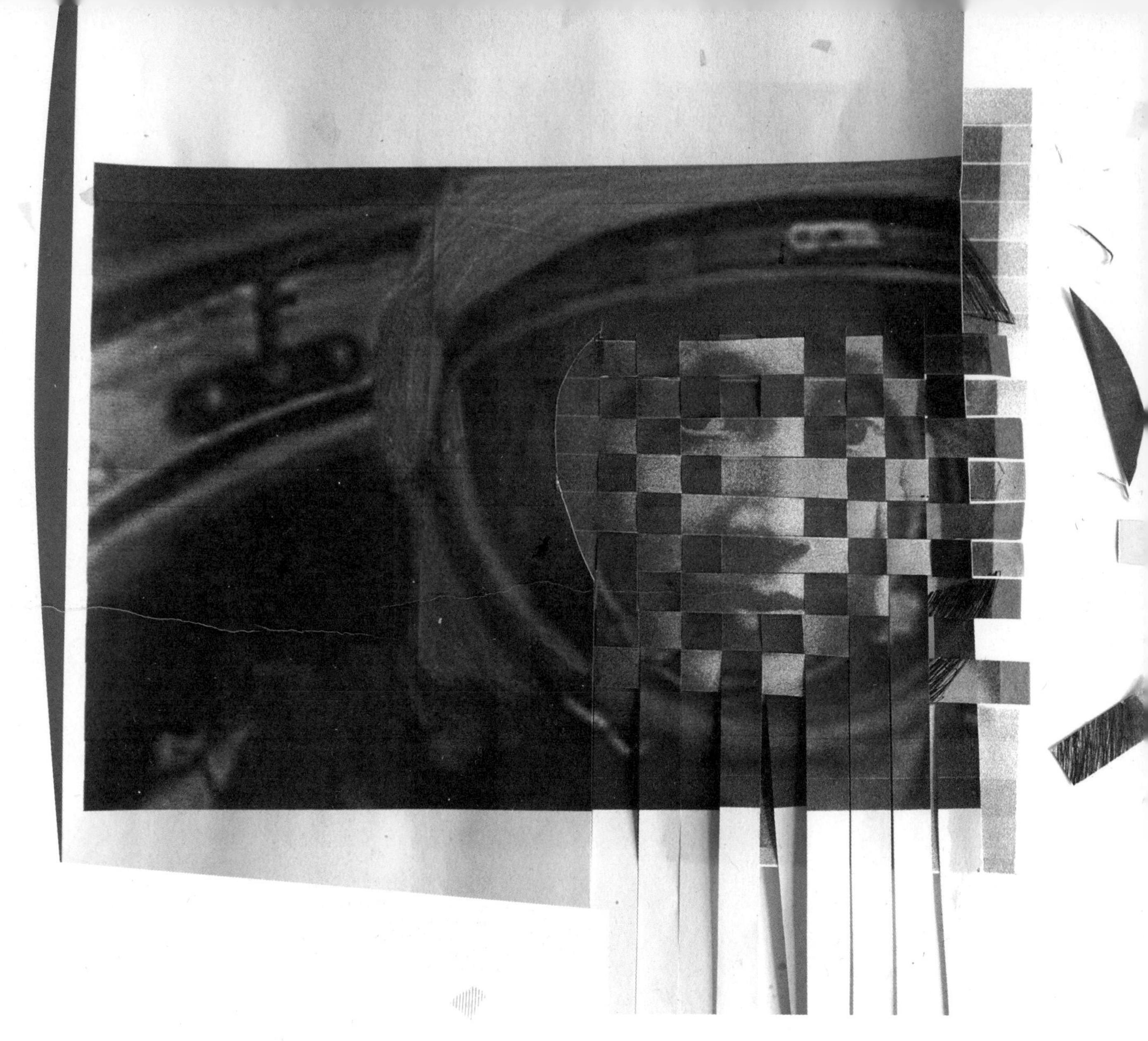

... This is part of our history, this is our defense.

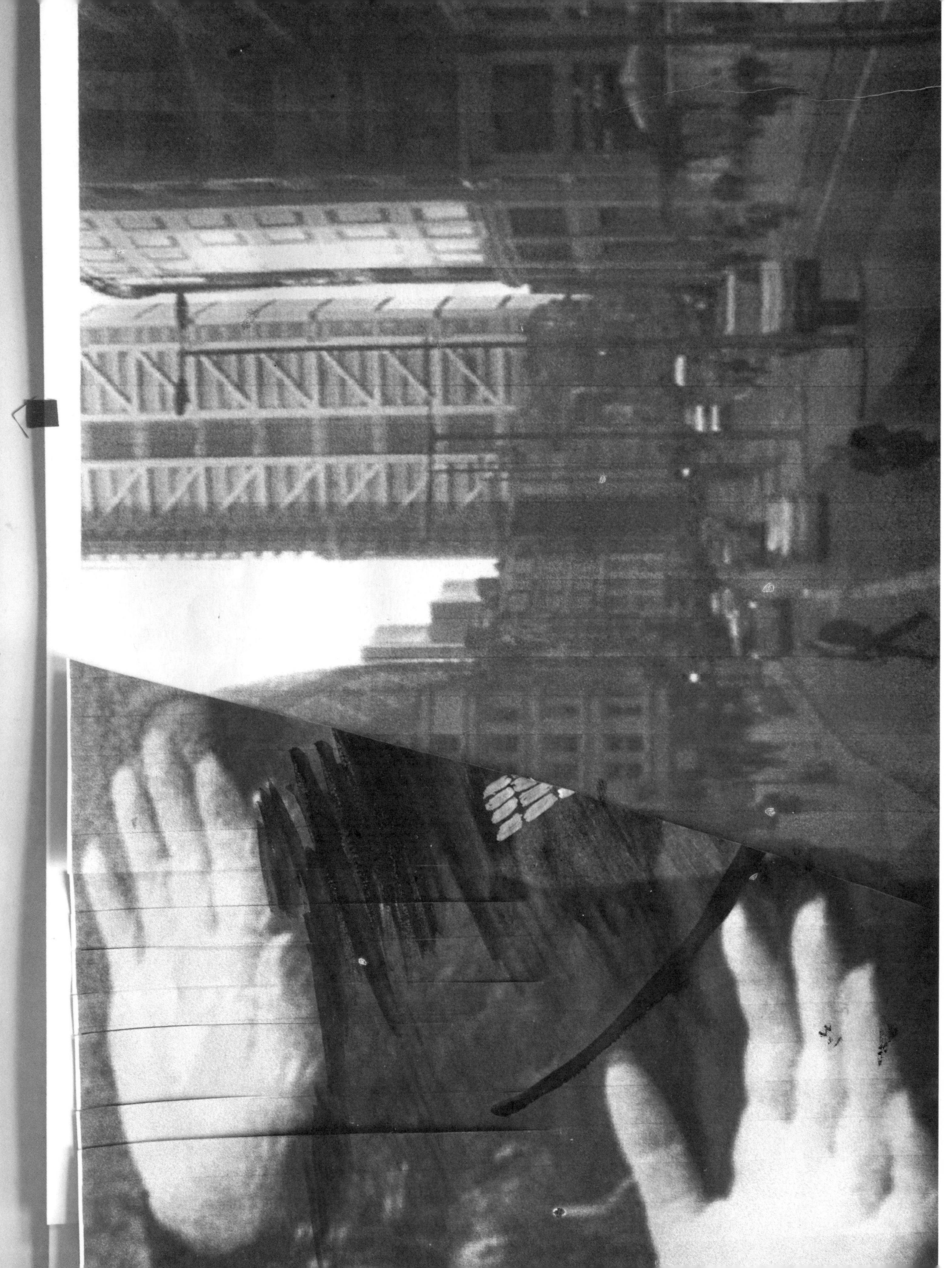

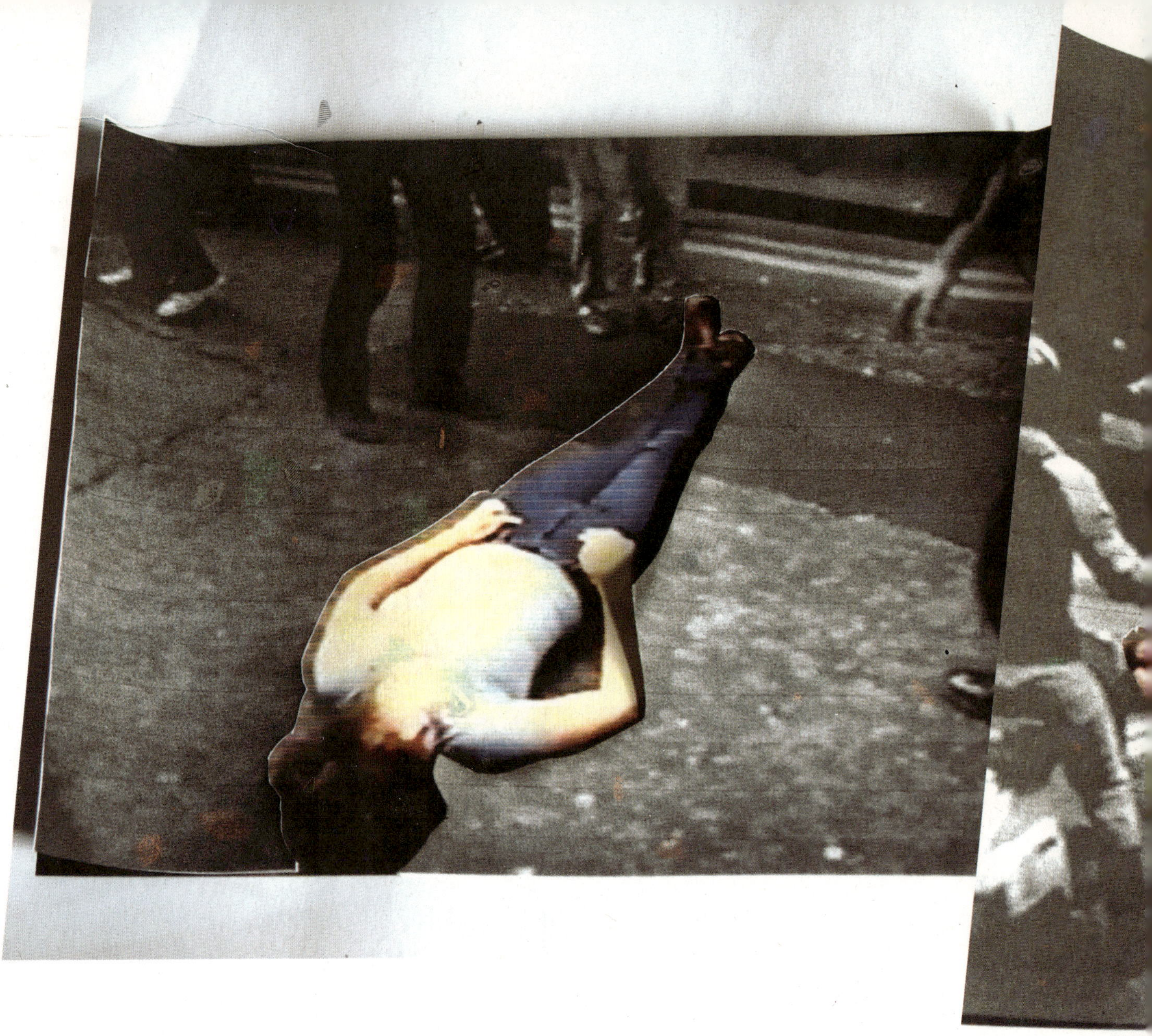

The camera moves to the right and up into the sun. Overexposure turns the film frames white. As the camera continues to the right we see the 'Die-in at the Stock Exchange'[15]. Groups of women lie Valie Export-like on the streets blocking the employees on their way to their offices. For a moment we are back to the political feminism and the City of London of the early 1980s.

15. Action by 'The Greenham Women' on the occasion of President Reagan's visit to the UK, the City of London, 1983.

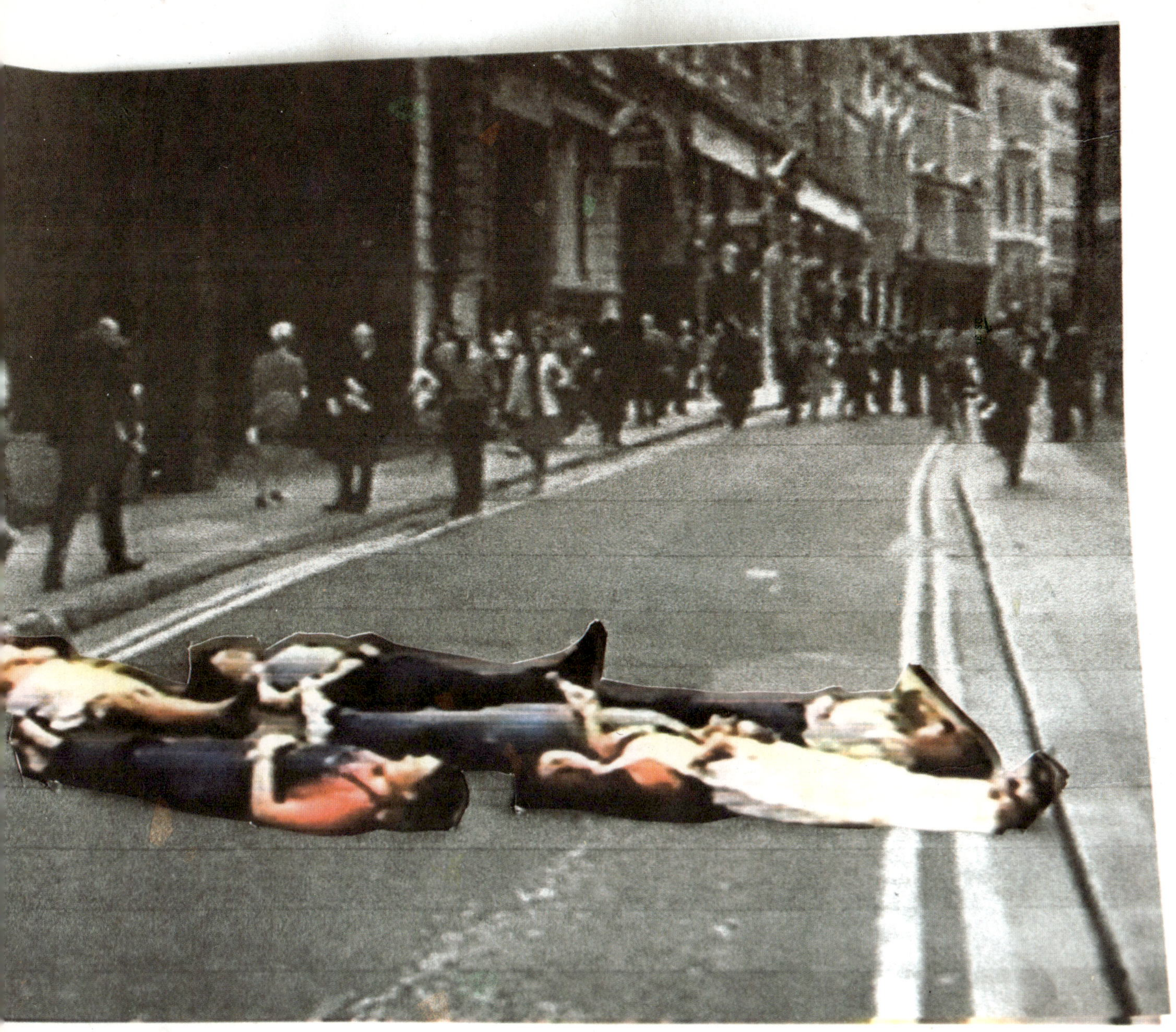

A cross dissolve transition returns us to the view from the bus, the City of 2012's near future
and Cosmo-Freedom fighter: *We want, we want people who are responsible for this mess
to face ... a ... an inquiry ... this is a story of deceit ... I'm sorry, this is really ... should go
away to Hollywood.*

The video loops.
////

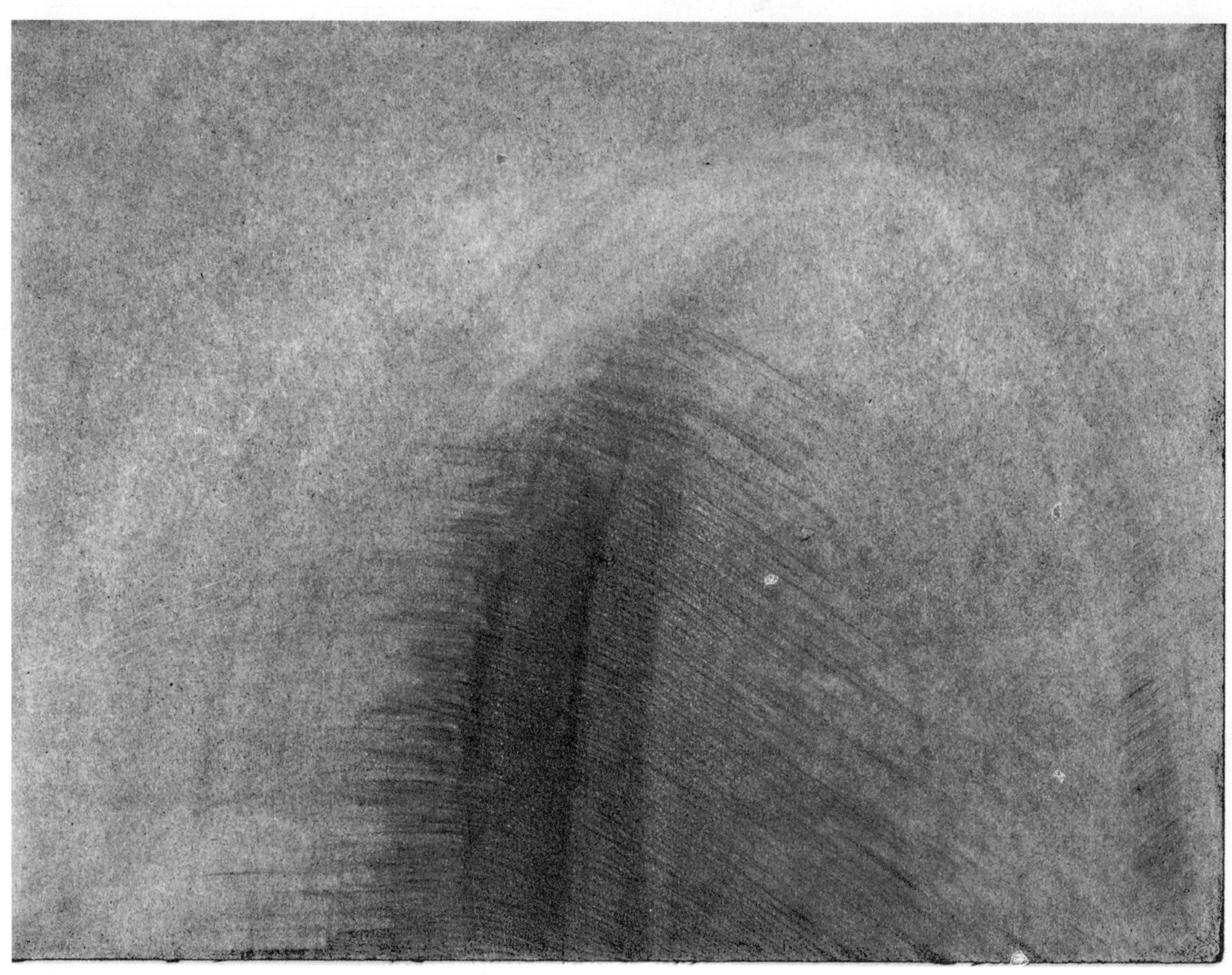

A-W-O-R-L-D-O-F-O-U-R-O-W-N
Eline McGeorge, 2012
www.elinemcgeorge.org
www.hollybushgardens.co.uk
ISBN 978-1-907908-05-7
Published in the UK in 2012 by Dent-De-Leone (www.dentdeleone.co.nz)
Edited by Malin Ståhl, designed by åbäke, printed by Aldgate Press (500 copies)
The text in this book is based on the video *A World Of Our Own*, Eline McGeorge, 2012.

Front cover: *Modified from the Pioneer Plaque* (1972), 2012
Back cover: *On Violence + In search for the post-capitalist self* (weave), 2012